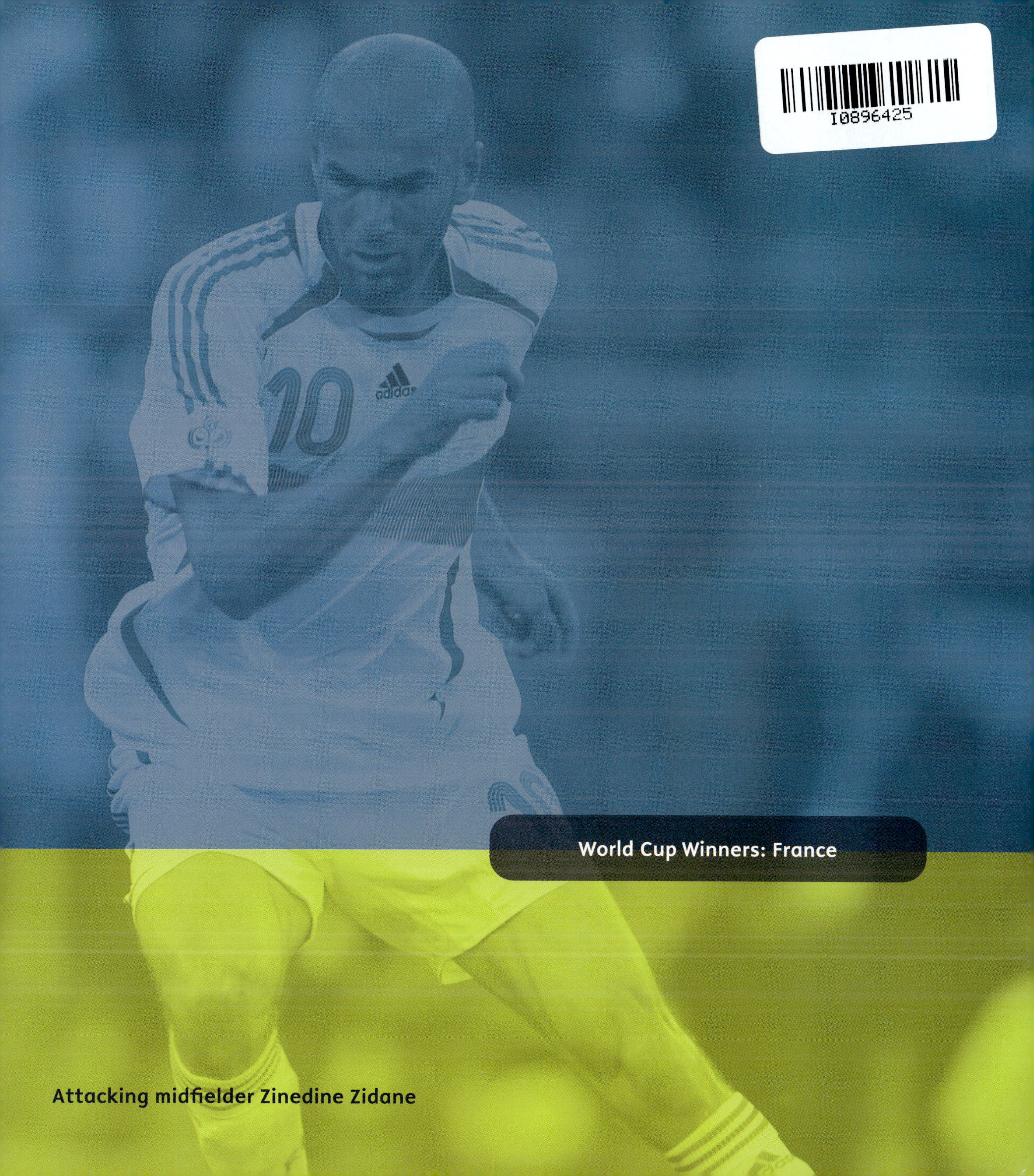

World Cup Winners: France

Attacking midfielder Zinedine Zidane

Midfielder Paul Pogba

WORLD CUP WINNERS

FRANCE

JAMES BARRY

CREATIVE SPORTS

CREATIVE EDUCATION / CREATIVE PAPERBACKS

Published by Creative Education and Creative Paperbacks
P.O. Box 227, Mankato, Minnesota 56002
Creative Education and Creative Paperbacks are imprints of
The Creative Company
www.thecreativecompany.us

Book design by Blue Design (www.bluedes.com)

Images by Getty Images/Alex Livesey - Danehouse, cover, 7, Chris Brunskill/Fantasista, 16, David Cannon, 6, Henri Szwarc, 15, Marco Canoniero, 3, 10, Michael Mayhew/Sportsphoto/Allstar, 5, Mike Egerton - EMPICS, 20, Richard Sellers/Allstar, 1, Ulrik Pedersen/NurPhoto, 2; Unsplash/cyril mzn, 9; Wikimedia Commons/Agence de presse Mondial Photo-Presse, 24, Henri Manuel, 4, public domain, 12, 19
Every effort has been made to contact copyright holders for material reproduced in this book. Any omissions will be rectified in subsequent printings if notice is given to the publisher.

Library of Congress Cataloging-in-Publication Data
Names: Barry, James, author.
Title: France / James Barry.
Description: Mankato, Minnesota : Creative Education and Creative Paperbacks, 2026. | Series: Creative sports. World Cup winners | Includes index. | Audience: Ages 7–10 | Audience: Grades 2–3 | Summary: "Led by legendary midfielder Zinedine Zidane and teen sensation Kylian Mbappé, France has won two FIFA World Cups. This elementary title follows "The Blue" as they kick their way into the hearts of fans worldwide"– Provided by publisher.
Identifiers: LCCN 2024046130 (print) | LCCN 2024046131 (ebook) | ISBN 9798889896012 (library binding) | ISBN 9781682777671 (paperback) | ISBN 9798889896814 (ebook)
Subjects: LCSH: Soccer–France–History–Juvenile literature. | Soccer teams–France–History–Juvenile literature. | World Cup (Soccer)–Juvenile literature.
Classification: LCC GV944.F8 B38 2026 (print) | LCC GV944.F8 (ebook) | DDC 796.334/660944–dc23/eng/20241208
LC record available at https://lccn.loc.gov/2024046130
LC ebook record available at https://lccn.loc.gov/2024046131

Printed in India

Defensive midfielder Didier Deschamps

Midfielder Michel Platini

CONTENTS

Home of the Team

France is the biggest country in western Europe. The capital of France is Paris. It's known as the "City of Light." It's home to the famous Eiffel Tower.

The most popular sport in France is soccer. Fans all over the country cheer on their national team. It's one of the few teams to have won the World Cup. The World Cup is a worldwide soccer tournament. Countries make teams of their best players. Every four years, they compete to become world champion.

Striker Olivier Giroud

Team Traditions

The France national team is known as "Les Bleus" ("The Blues") for its blue jersey. The team's symbol is the rooster. The players have worn it on their jerseys for more than 100 years. One of France's biggest **rivals** is Germany. They're two of the most successful national teams in the world. They've played each other more than 30 times.

The France national team in 1904

Team History

France played its first match in 1904. It was a **friendly** against Belgium in front of 1,500 people. Jules Rimet was the leader of French soccer. He played a big part in creating the World Cup. The World Cup trophy was named the Jules Rimet trophy in his honor.

In 1930, France scored the first goal in World Cup history. France had many great teams for many years. But it did not make its first World Cup final until 1998. It beat Brazil 3–0 in its home stadium in Paris. Legendary midfielder Zinedine Zidane was the Man of the Match. France made another World Cup final in 2006. But it lost to Italy in penalty kicks. Zidane was ejected from the match for headbutting an opponent.

Attacking midfielder Zinedine Zidane

Striker Kylian Mbappé

In 2018, France won its second World Cup. It beat Croatia 4–2 in the final. Young **striker** Kylian Mbappé became only the second teenager, after Brazil legend Pelé, to score in a World Cup final. Mbappé led the team to another World Cup final in 2022. He scored a **hat trick** against Argentina. But France lost the match in penalty kicks. It was one of the most exciting finals in World Cup history.

Team Stars

France has had many great stars in its history. Just Fontaine scored 13 goals at the 1958 World Cup. That is still the most ever scored by one player in one World Cup. **Playmaker** Michel Platini was one of the finest passers ever. He won the **Ballon d'Or** three times in a row in the 1980s.

Striker Just Fontaine

FRANCE

Striker Thierry Henry

Didier Deschamps captained France to its first World Cup in 1998. In 2018, Deschamps won the World Cup as coach. He is only the third player ever to achieve it. Striker Thierry Henry was French Player of the Year a record five times. Mbappé is still France's best player. Fans hope he will help bring another World Cup to France soon.

About the France National Team

First year: 1904

Team colors: dark blue, blue, red, white

Home stadium: Stade de France

WORLD CUP VICTORIES:

1998, 3–0 over Brazil

2018, 4–2 over Croatia

TEAM WEBSITE:

https://uk.fff.fr/

Glossary

Ballon d'Or — an award given every year to the world's best soccer player

friendly — a game outside a tournament

hat trick — when a player scores three goals in a single match

playmaker — a player who controls the flow of play and makes passes leading to goals

rival — a team that plays extra hard against another team

striker — a player who mainly attacks and scores goals, rather than defends

Jules Rimet

Index